bedbugdot™
early-warning detection system

Find the Spot…

Apply the Dot!

Written exclusively for bedbugdot by:

Denise Donovan
Founder/Director

The International Bed Bug Resource Authority
The Most Trusted Name in
Bed Bug Education and Resources

ISBN-10:0989521796
ISBN-13:978-0-9895217-9-6
Book Design: Competitive Edge Group
Manufactured in the United States
Printed by: On Demand
Photographs used with permission by: IBBRA, Richard Naylor PhD, Lou Sorkin BCE and David Mora

DISCLAIMER

This publication is intended to provide helpful and informative material on the subject of bed bugs. It is sold with the understanding that the author and publisher are not engaged in rendering any professional services through this book other than education. The reader should consult his or her pest management professional before adopting any of the suggestions in this book or drawing inferences from it. This book is not intended in any way to be a substitute for professional pest management advice or treatment for bed bugs.

Never disregard professional medical advice or delay in seeking it because of something you have read in this book when it comes to bed bug health related problems. This book is written with the intention of public awareness on bed bugs and important information that people need to know.

The author and publisher specifically disclaim all responsibility for any liability, injury, loss, or risk, personal or otherwise, which is incurred as a consequence, directly or indirectly, of the use and application of any of the contents of this book.

INTRODUCTION

Congratulations on purchasing your bedbugdot early-warning detection system. You certainly wouldn't go into battle without a plan and dealing with bed bugs without information and awareness can be the same thing. This will be one of the most important books you will ever read to help you understand that bed bugs are becoming a way of life and since they are literally everywhere it is only a matter of time when you should have one introduced to your life.

Since these are pests we have lived without for many years, it's going to take time and effort on everyone's part to increase awareness and be "proactive and preventative" in their approach with bed bugs. This is pertinent information you need so they don't take up residence with you.

You will learn the many "risk" factors starting with the fact that bed bugs need blood to exist and you just happen to have it.

Once bed bugs take up residence and go unnoticed for time, it takes a lot of hard work and money to regain control. Early detection plays the most significant role, as without educated and informed consumers, control cannot be easily achieved.

This book was written for easy comprehension as a bonus to purchasing the bedbugdot system. It helps you understand the nature of the bed bug and why they are one of, if not the toughest pests ever to eliminate. Along with identifying them, you will learn where they hide, ways of detecting them, travel tips and plenty of prevention methods.

Especially important you will learn valuable tips on what not to do if you should encounter bed bugs.

The bedbugdot website has a multitude of environmental illustrations with proper placement areas of common bed bug hiding places to assist you. www.bedbugdot.com

If you should have any questions, feel free to reach out to one of our knowledgeable agents for help. 844-823-3284 or 844-9-bedbugdot

TABLE OF CONTENTS

CHAPTER 1

CHAPTER 2

CHAPTER 3

CHAPTER 4

CHAPTER 1

THE BED BUGS JOURNEY

Bed bugs dated as far back as cave dwellers many centuries ago. The earliest historical citations go back to 423 B.C. Populations were small; and travel was limited to foot.

INTERNATIONAL TRAVEL

As populations grew, new means and ways of travel moved people from foot to mules, horses with carriages, to autos and trains, buses, boats, ships, and airplanes. What once took early settlers months to travel is now moving millions of people across the countries and continents in record speed. This constant travel carries bed bugs from homes to homes, business-to-business, city to city and country to country. They now have become a common pest with great significance worldwide.

THE BANNING OF CHEMICALS

Chlorinated Hydrocarbon/known as DDT (originally used for control of malaria and typhus), was introduced as a major advancement in bed bug control in the late 1930's.

In 1962, an American Biologist, Rachel Carson wrote a book that brought immediate concern to address the toxic effects of DDT. Her book Silent Spring helped change history. In her book, she adamantly questioned the logic behind the continuous use of and release of these chemicals into the environment. This soon became the birth of the environmental movement.

On December 2, 1970, under President Richard Nixon, The Environmental Protection Agency (EPA) was formed. The results of a large public outcry eventually led to DDT being banned in the US in 1972.

CHEMICAL RESISTANCE

Chemical resistance has been known about for many years and the signs of it with bed bugs continue to show. It doesn't mean that all strains of bed bugs are resistant to all chemicals though.

A WHOLE GENERATION HAS NEVER SEEN A BED BUG

Unless you lived back in the thirties, we have lived for many years without these pests. Many people still believe "Sleep tight, don't let the bed bugs bite", was some sort of nursery rhyme from years ago. Beginning in the late 1990's, the numbers of new sightings and severities of bed bug infestations began to grow significantly throughout the world.

The standard acceptable rules, strategies and management methods for pest control were not working. This left the pest control industry trying to figure out how to eliminate them by pulling products from their arsenals used for other pests. Many of these trial and error techniques were failing miserably.

PEOPLE NOT AFFECTED BY BED BUG BITES

There are people that have reactions to bed bug bites. However, there are those who can get bit repeatedly and have little to no reactions to the bite. Some people can get bit and do not show signs for a week or more.

LACK OF SOCIETAL EDUCATION

Society as a whole is feeling the financial economic burden of bed bug infestations. Increasing daily, the economic losses from treatments, replacement of belongings, health care, lost wages, lost business revenues and reduced productivity are quite substantial.

Now take an insect that has been missing from our society for many years, travels easily, has resistance to some chemicals; add questionable training of some pest management, with people that are not affected by bites, that are exponentially growing, and now you have a "perfect storm" for disaster.

Bed bugs do not care if you are rich or poor and they do not care whether your house is clean or dirty. They only want your blood.

CHAPTER 2

WHAT ARE BED BUGS?

Bed bugs, scientifically known as Cimex lectularius (Hemiptera: Cimicidae) are small insects that are flattened dorsally. They do not jump or fly. Bed bugs feed upon warm blood, and we as humans are perfect hosts.

PROPER IDENTIFICATION IS CRITICAL

It is very important to know what bed bugs look like compared to similar insects as the treatment options and costs are very different. Adult bed bugs are reddish brown in color, and are approximately ¼ inch in length. The adults can be easily seen with the naked eye.

DEVELOPMENTAL STAGES OF THE BED BUG

Regardless of what you have read, bed bug eggs are pearl white, translucent in color and similar to the size of a poppy seed and are not very visible to the human eye. A female bed bug can lay hundreds of these eggs in her lifetime, (regular feedings and mating are required).

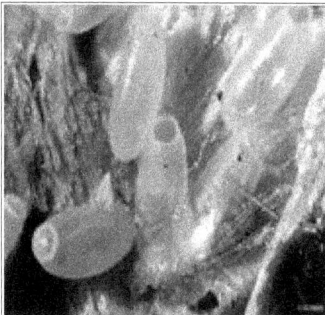

The eggs are attached to surfaces by a sticky substance and depending on temperature and conditions, these eggs can hatch anywhere from three to ten days or longer.

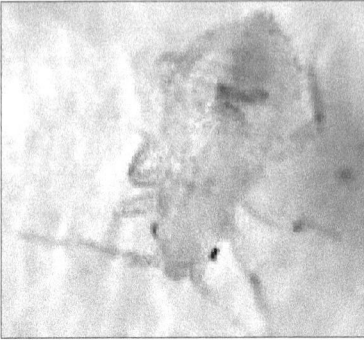

The immature bed bug (nymph) is translucent, pearl whitish in color and become slightly darker with each stage as they reach maturity.

The bed bug develops through five of these immature stages before reaching the adult reproduction stage.

The young nymph may not always be easy to see, but after a nymph feeds, the blood inside shows through their pale skin.

Fully fed, the bed bug takes on the shape of a torpedo or football with an elongated trunk that is bright red in color. As digestion progresses, the blood turns darker and the bug flattens out due to voiding until its next blood meal.

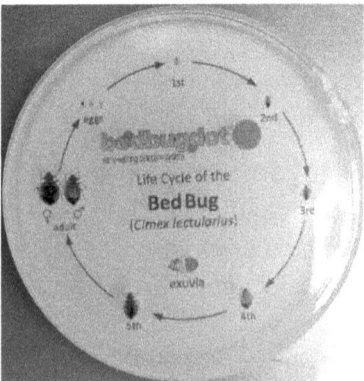

The time for development from first nymph to adult varies according to temperature, blood meals and conditions. (approximately 22 to 36 days)

During this developmental growth period, they shed their skin (or molt) as they grow to the next stage.

Each stage, from 1st instar nymph to adult, has to take at least one blood meal in order to continue through the next successive stage to the adult bed bug.

The adult bed bugs have been reported to have ability to survive from 4 months to 2 years depending on regular access to blood meals and favorable temperatures.

During feeding status, bed bugs look very different. An unfed bed bug looks more like a flat disk but increase to approximately 3 to 4 times that of their original size after a blood meal.

REPRODUCTION

Bed bugs can lay hundreds of eggs in their lifetime, in which regular feeding and mating are always required. Large populations of bed bugs take time to develop, but if a few female adults are not detected early, you could well have thousands after 3 or 4 months!

PHYSICAL SIGNS OF BED BUGS

FECAL STAINS (POOP)

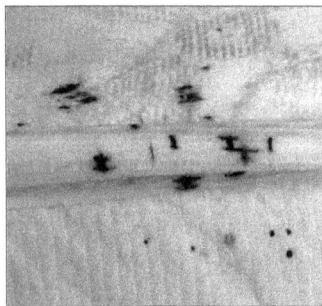

These stains appear to be minute "ink dots", (like from a black marker pen). The larger the infestation, the greater amount of these will be found. Some materials are "impervious to moisture" and the dropping may "bead up" on the surface.

MOLTED BED BUG SKINS (CASTINGS)

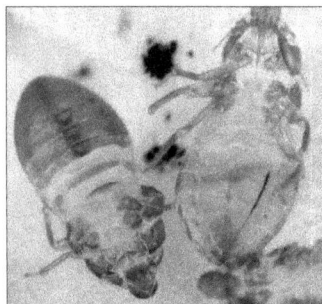

The bed bug grows out of its skin and leaves the old one behind. They are normally a paper-thin opaque duplication of the bed bug. Depending on how long you have had an infestation, you may find different "sizes" as each stage of growth to maturity is a little larger than the last.

BLOOD SPOTS

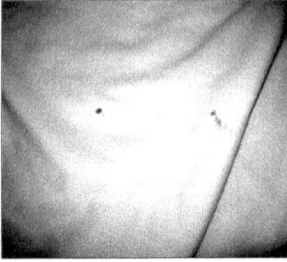

Outside of bite marks, people may find blood spots. These spots may be recognized as rusty spots on bedclothes, sheets, furniture and surrounding walls.

PECULIAR ODOR

These odors are mostly associated with higher numbers of bed bugs and longer infestations, and like any of the normal human smells and scents, if you reside in the room on a regular basis you may be "use to" the smell.

BED BUG BITES AND FEEDING HABITS

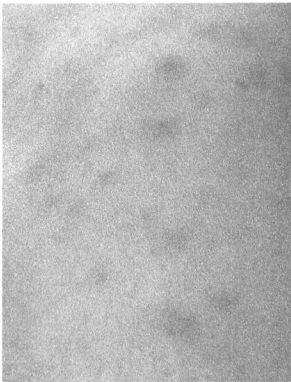

Bed bugs are drawn by warm temperature, carbon dioxide and are known to feed on exposed skin while you are sleeping. Nevertheless, bed bugs can feed at any time of the day or night whether you are sleeping or not and adjust their feeding time to adapt to the host's sleeping patterns.

They will bite any exposed area of the body, face, neck, arms, and hands. The act of biting is usually not felt.

For some people, the first sign of a bed bug problem may be waking up with unidentified bites. These bites resembles those caused by many other kinds of blood feeding insects and can rarely be identified by the appearance of the bites alone. In order to identify the bites as bed bugs the culprit "must be found".

A common concern is whether they transmit diseases. The bed bug has not been known to transmit diseases but they are known for reducing the quality of life of the bite victim.

The number of bites <u>does not always</u> mean there are large amounts of bed bugs involved. Bed bugs are sensitive to any type of movement or slightest disturbance and may withdraw its mouthparts during the feeding, move a short distance and continue to feed again. This may cause multiple bites that may be in a row. This is sometimes called a "Breakfast – Lunch – and Dinner" pattern. Two people sharing the same bed can be affected differently.

TREATING BED BUG BITES

Most bites do not require any medical treatment and will go away with time. However, bed bug bites can be pretty itchy. Constant scratching creates a cycle, which causes the "itchy area" to spread, and healing takes longer than if you avoid scratching.

To relieve the itchiness there are many over-the-counter (OTC) creams and lotions available. (E.g. *Calamine Lotion, Hydrocortisone Cream, Lanacane, Dermarest Plus, Gold Bond Anti-itch, Benzocane*)

- Hot water tends to increase the "itchiness". Use tepid water when bathing or showering.

- Young children have a hard time not scratching the bites. To help avoid opening the skin, keep their fingernails short and place socks on their hands.

NOTE: Call the doctor if you see any signs of an allergic reaction, or infection. Never disregard professional medical advice or delay seeking it because of something you have read in this book when it comes to any bed bug health related problem or remedy.

CHAPTER 3

OK, so you now know what a bed bug looks like in all stages of development – but do you know what it looks like when hidden away in your home, office or personal belongings?

As their name implies, bed bugs are commonly associated with areas where we sleep or relax. But don't put it past the bed bug to be found outside resting areas. They can be found in dressers, chair cushions, sofas, behind electrical outlets, in folds of draperies, clocks, phones, shoes, cracks and crevices, under carpet tacks, around baseboards, picture frames, under the bed, in books, door hinges, light fixtures, in wheelchairs and in or under any clutter or objects near a bed, lounging area or work station.

If you suspect bed bugs you must be extremely thorough during the inspection process and be sure not to rush through. **NEVER REMOVE** anything from the suspected premise you are inspecting. If you removed any item, it must be bagged and sealed properly.

During inspection, avoid sitting, leaning or placing anything on beds or couches or chairs. Bed bugs may be in different stages during your investigation. Do not be discouraged, in a short period of time you will be trained to look for certain telltale signs that improve your chances of finding them.

Tools that can make your search easier include a flashlight, a magnifying glass, a screwdriver (for disassembling items) and sealable plastics bags in several sizes.

BEDS

Look on your bedspread, blanket, duvet, throw pillows (do not forget teddy bears or any other stuffed animals or toys), or any other covering you may have on your bed. Examine your sheets and pillowcases, too.

Pull the bed out and away from the wall and remove the headboard. Carefully examine the headboard front and back for any bed bug signs.

MATTRESS AND BOX SPRINGS

Carefully examine the surfaces paying close attention to folds and depressions. Then move on to the piping (both upper and lower sides) around the edges of the mattress using the flashlight. If the mattress has buttons, examine them for any signs. Flip the mattress and examine the same on the other side. Sometimes they crawl into the mattress through grommets or tears and cuts.

Examine the box springs. On the back of the box spring is a fabric stapled in place that has to be removed. Bed bugs love to crawl inside the box spring between the staples. Carefully check for bed bugs where the material is folded under around the edges. Using a flathead screwdriver, remove the back material, then carefully examine the inside wood frame as well as outside using your flashlight.

Using the LED light and magnifying glass to look close in closets and dresser drawers, couches, loveseats, pullout beds, recliners and easy chairs, all other non-washable items, curtain, shutters and blinds, electrical items and outlets, animal bedding.

LAUNDRY TIPS

If you should discover bed bugs, plan to spend a lot of time doing laundry for all clothing and fabrics. You must be careful while transporting <u>anything</u> out from the infected room(s). Wash and dry these items on HOT and place them into sealed bags or sealed storage bins and set aside. Do not bring these back into the room you are treating. (You can use a garage, porch or basement). It is not necessary to wash all items. Items that are clean can be placed directly into a hot dryer for 40-55 minutes, bagged and set aside.

DON'T OVER PACK CLOTHING IN TUB OR DRYER
LOOSLY FIT SO ALL ITEMS GET HOT

DISCARDING ITEMS

In most cases, it is not necessary to dispose of furniture, prior to treatment. In fact, depending on the size of the infestation, the condition and age of the furniture, most infested furniture can be cleaned and treated. If you must discard anything, DO NOT DO IT without wrapping and marking it. In many cases, the money spent on replacing furniture might be better spent on professional treatment.

Whenever discarding items be sure to wrap, seal and mark items (BED BUG INFESTED), before disposal. Someone's trash is another's treasure and can fall into the hands of someone who now brings bed bugs into their home spreading the infestation throughout the community.

ADDING NEW FURNITURE

If you made the decision to discard any furniture items and need replacement – do not replace anything until your treatment is 100% successful. You risk infesting your new furniture and having to start treatment all over again.

FINDING A QUALIFIED PEST PROFESSIONAL

If you find bed bugs, take it serious! Always deal with a qualified bed bug pest management company. Qualified companies have intensive training, tools and experience to deal with the nature of the bed bug. This is not the time to hire a company without bed bug experience, take the cheapest bid or use anyone without proper training and experience.

Choosing a professional pest control company is an important decision. Not all companies are experienced in bed bug elimination. It is imperative that you search for experienced bed bug professionals who have a track record of success with bed bugs. Don't just open the yellow pages and call on the largest ad, take time to do your homework first! For help finding a qualified company you can always depend upon the IBBRA www.ibbra.org or 888-966-2332

BEST BED BUG DETECTION TOOLS

BEDBUGDOT -The *bedbugdot* is cost effective and well suited for helping you discover bed bugs in early stages. Because common bed bug hot spots are shown, people find it easier to place the dots in these areas and check them often. **NOTE:** The *bedbugdot* was not designed to eliminate or treat a bed bug infested area, only to provide shelter, create awareness and detect the presence of bed bugs.

BED BUG DETECTION DOGS -Trained experts detect bed bugs for a living but they must find actual live bed bugs and/or eggs. This laborious project may take hours of searching for humans whereas these dogs sweep through in record speed. The effectiveness of a dog team is greater in comparison to that of a human technician alone.

PREVENTING BED BUGS

CLEANING UP THE CLUTTER - Bed bugs are experts at hiding and finding them can present quite a challenge. Heavily cluttered dwellings create a million and one places for bed bugs to hide. Having clutter can cause complete failure of bed bug treatments. If you have piles of boxes, newspapers, magazines or just "stuff", it's time you clean it up. Doing this will take away many harborage areas and make it easier to find them.

BEDS AND LOUNGING AREAS

Change your bed linens regularly; check your bedbugdots often for any signs. Always examine piping on mattresses and box springs for early signs. Vacuum couches, chairs and carpets regularly.

MAKING HOUSEHOLD REPAIRS

Take away as many possible harborages for bed bugs. Separations between baseboards, grout, seams of wallpaper, crown molding, door jams. Clear silicone fills these areas so bed bugs cannot enter. Consider replacing worn carpeting with tile; and because bed bugs travel along routes created by pipes, cables and electrical conduits, seal any openings where pipes, wires or other utilities come into your home.

MISCELLANEOUS PREVENTION POINTERS

Avoid shopping at thrift stores, pawnshops, and Craig's list. Be mindful of anything borrowed or given to you or discarded furniture or mattresses found at the curbside. Any of these items should be thoroughly inspected for bed bugs before bringing them into your home.

Use a large plastic self-locking bag to contain items like computer bags, purses, jackets, backpacks and lunch boxes when transporting them back and forth from work, school or places visited. Be sure to inspect all items a visitor may bring into your home or workplace. These include family, out of town guests, neighbors, maintenance and service people, delivery people, sales clerk, and social workers.

TRAVEL TIPS SO YOU DON'T BRING HOME BED BUG SOUVENIRS

Wrap and seal your belongings and luggage in plastic bags that can be removed upon arrival. Re-wrap with fresh new plastic before returning home. Consider using soft fabric duffle bags. These can easily be thrown into a hot dryer once your trip is over to kill any possible hitchhikers.

SAFEGUARDING YOUR BELONGINGS AT HOTELS

Leave your luggage and belongings outside the room, in your car, place them in the shower, or tub until your bed bug inspection is complete.

After your inspection, still consider not placing your luggage or belongings on the bed or soft chairs and couches. Hang your clothing in the middle of the clothing rack and place luggage on the luggage rack (after checking for bed bugs) Do not place clothing in drawers without being in a sealed plastic bag. Avoid placing your shoes under the bed or laying clothing on the bed, couch or chairs.

PRECAUTIONS FOR RETURNING HOME

No matter how careful we are, the possibility of a bed bug "souvenir" latching on is always there. To be sure, unpack in your garage or an area outside your dwelling.

Remove bagged clothing for proper cleaning and thoroughly vacuum or steam clean your luggage. If you have a duffle bag, place it in a hot dryer for 40-60 minutes.

LUGGAGE DECONTAMINATION DEVICES

These are great for those who travel or anyone who suspects bed bugs after visiting a friend, school or work. Safely heating contents up to over 120ºF for a sustained period will kill bed bugs. www.zappbug.com

MATTRESS ENCASEMENTS

Of course there are other reasons other than bed bugs to place a protective cover on our beds. They protect against sweat, spills, bed wetting, incontinence problems, allergies and dust mites.

Most importantly they protect your investment assuring you get years of use and can easily be removed for cleaning and replacement.

Because bed bugs love the crevices along the piping and seams of mattresses, and love hiding deep in the areas of box springs, a good quality encasement designed for bed bugs, keep them from invading and helps to avoid having to treat them.

Ultimate Bedding USA mattress and box springs encasements provide extra protection against bed bugs while protecting your investment against many other soil, stains and bugs and come with a Lifetime Warranty. http://www.acespestsolutions.com/shop-aces/

DAILY BED BUG AWARENESS

- Check for bed bugs and signs of them on a regular basis using bedbugdot to insure you don't miss spots.
- Develop a thorough weekly routine of vacuuming, change sheets, and more importantly remove clutter.
- Protect your mattress and box springs with good quality mattress encasements.
- Pay extra attention to where you could "pick up" the hitchhikers.
- Take extra precautions when traveling.
- If you suspect or find bed bugs call a professional as soon as possible!

WHAT NOT TO DO

- Do not ignore bed bugs; they don't go away on their own.
- Do not move infested bedding, furniture or clothing to other rooms in the home.
- Do not donate infested items to charities or thrift stores.
- Do not use pesticides in your home.
- Do not replace mattresses or furniture before you eliminate EVERY possible bed bug!!!!
- Do not use a hair dryer. Will blow bugs all over the place!
- Don't send your infested clothing to a dry cleaner without asking or advising them first!

CAUTION: It is not advisable for homeowners to attempt to treat for bed bug infestations on their own. They will likely become dispersed, resulting in a more expensive and difficult treatment later on.

If you live in rented property and discover bed bugs with your bedbugdot early-warning system, always seek help from property owner and do not attempt to self-treat, you may spread them to adjoining units.

CHAPTER 4

Q: Why should I inspect for bed bugs?

Bed bugs can go unnoticed for long periods. Since they have an impressive reproductive cycle, discovering bed bugs during the early introduction phase keeps infestations from developing. Ongoing inspection is part of a proactive lifestyle and is critical to protecting against a potential infestation.

Q: What is a bedbugdot?

The bedbugdot is a discrete, maintenance-free, early-warning detection system, developed to help people become aware of the presence of bed bugs before an infestation can develop.

Made from 100% recycled materials, the bedbugdot is environmentally safe and contains no chemicals, glues or attractants to hurt or harm children or pets.

Q: How do bedbugdots come packaged?

Environments come in different sizes and so does bedbugdot. From large multi-bed hotels to a one-bed apartment, bedbugdot comes packaged in three convenient sizes to fit the needs of homeowners and apartment dwellers, commercial buildings and professional pest control.

- Home Pack (24 units) Great for Studios, One and Two Bedroom Apartments and small Homes.

- Pro Pack (100 units) Great for Homes, Daycare, Small Businesses.

- Commercial Pack (500 units) Hotels, Schools, Hospitals, Office Cubicles, etc.

Q: What are the three functions bedbugdot provides?

The bedbugdot provides:

- 24-hour Bed bug awareness within ones surroundings!
- Teaches you bed bug hot spots!
- Detects bed bugs early before an infestation can build!

#1 Creates 24-hour Awareness:

Some people go months before discovering they have bed bugs. The bedbugdot draws people to awareness by having them look for signs of bed bugs more often than without them. All you have to remember is to check them.

#2 Learn Bed Bug Hot Spots:

Because of the bed bugs size and hidden nature, they often go unnoticed for great periods which is why it leads to infestation levels. Bedbugdot assists you in knowing these favorite hiding places assuring you never miss a spot.

#3 Detect Bed Bugs Early:

The bedbugdot early-warning system is easily checked for signs of bed bugs. We have "Find the Spot and Apply the Dot" environments to show you common Hot Spots where bed bugs like to hide. With bedbugdots in place, you can examine those areas often enough so an infestation does not build.

NOTE: Not intended as a trap or monitor to prevent, destroy, repel or mitigate any pest.

Q: How do I know where to install the bedbugdot?

Since bed bugs are so good at hitchhiking they are carried into many different environments including, homes, apartments, doctor and hospital waiting rooms, cubicles at work, school, church, social gathering halls, public transportation vehicles, restaurants, libraries, and more. Install bedbugdot in areas where people come together, sit or rest for extended time.

Bedbugdot provides easy to understand, visual environment layouts on their web site, which shows you the most common places bed bugs hide. www.bedbugdot.com Visit our site often for continued bed bug education.

Note: These environment layouts show **ALL POSSIBLE BED BUG HOT SPOTS**. You need not place a bedbugdot in every area shown on the layouts. Only areas where you know are commonly occupied.

Q: What are signs that I may have bed bugs?

- Mysterious or unexplained bites
- Any live insects
- Any dark spots (Fecal spots)
- Cast skins (yellow or white paper-thin bed bug skins)
- Eggs

Outside of visual signs, some people show reactions to the bite after a bed bug feeds. Bites can itch severely. Another sign can be a blood smear on bedding or clothing if a person squishes a bed bug with a full blood meal or scratches at a bite wound.

Q: How do I inspect the Bedbugdot?

Some signs of bed bugs may be obvious at a glance. Look closely around the bedbugdot, on the outside or middle of the bedbugdot, use a flashlight to inspect the complete area in and around the dot and surrounding

Q: When should I call in a professional?

If you notice any bed bug activity or signs in, on or around the bedbugdot.

Contact your Bed Bug Professional promptly showing the area you found it in for a complete inspection and evaluation. Replace bedbugdot after treatment for continuous early-warning detection.

Q: How often should I inspect bedbugdot?

Daily: Someone is being bitten regularly, hotels, nursing homes, hospital and doctor waiting rooms or previously infested premise.

Weekly: Frequent travelers and following a treatment

Monthly: General monitoring, homes, businesses, tenants or apartment living (anywhere for ongoing early detection)

Q: How many do I need?

Bedbugdot can cover many different locations and settings. Depending upon the amount of furniture, bedbugdot can serve as a reminder to check areas of high risk such as, schools, offices, churches, public gathering places, etc. or in home situations when a person travels often, has numerous people residing in the dwelling or frequent visitors. Visit our web site to see visual environment layouts for your convenience at www.bedbugdot.com

Q: Can I always be sure I will find bed bugs using the bedbugdot?

The reason bed bugs turn into "infestation" levels is that most people don't look for signs; especially those who don't show a reaction to the bites of a bed bug.

If you place bedbugdots in frequently used bed bug "hot spots" throughout your home or business and check those areas on a regular basis, if bed bugs have been introduced, you will find bed bugs or signs of them early enough to manage the situation before it grows.

NOTE: The key to bed bugs is finding them as early as you can. The bedbugdot is not designed or intended as a "monitor or trap", only as an awareness tool to assist you in knowing early to avoid a costly infestation.

Keeping track of when you last checked for bed bugs is a smart thing to do for all homes and businesses. Knowing when you first discovered signs of bed bugs can help in assisting pest control develop the best treatment for the situation.

The bedbugdot website provides a printable twelve month calendar where you can keep track of when you check your bedbugdots for signs.

Daily, weekly or monthly, with bedbugdot you will not miss a spot!

Download and print this handy calendar off our web site www.bedbugdot.com

Jan | Feb | Mar | April

May | June | July | Aug

Sept | Oct | Nov | Dec

This handy printable calendar serves as a reminder and makes it easy to keep track when you check for signs of bed bugs. Whether daily, weekly or monthly, your bedbugdot will give you peace of mind to avoid an infestation.

i